Parents Who Help Their Children Overcome Drugs

Lowell House Los Angeles
Contemporary Books Chicago

Parents
Who Help
Their Children
Overcome
~~~~~ Drugs ~~~~~

Barbara Cottman Becnel

Library of Congress Cataloging in Publication Data

Becnel, Barbara Cottman.
Parents who help their children overcome drugs / Barbara Cottman
Becnel.

Bibliography: p.
Includes index.
ISBN 0–929923–00–6
1. Children—United States—Drug use.   2. Drug abuse—United
States—Prevention.   3. Parenting—United States.   I. Title.
HV5824.C45B43   1989
649'.4—dc19   89–30297
CIP

Lowell House
1950 Sawtelle Blvd.
Los Angeles, CA 90025

Design: Barbara Monahan
Manufactured in the United States of America
10 9 8 7 6 5 4 3 2 1

This book is for my son and sister who have helped me learn how to forgive and, thus, love myself.

Contents

Acknowledgments

I am grateful for the consummate talent of my editor, Janice Gallagher, who has helped me look better on paper than I could ever have imagined. A thank-you is in order as well for Jack Artenstein, my publisher, who demonstrated faith by providing me with the opportunity to write this book. I am appreciative of the patience and understanding displayed by my "daytime" boss, Daniel J. Flaming, whenever I showed up for work a little bleary-eyed from having stayed up late to write the night before. I want to acknowledge my good fortune to have such a close friend as Paula Manning, who continues to encourage me every step of the way.

Last, I want to offer a special thanks to my parents. Each one played a role in shaping my character: My mother is responsible for the tenacity and confidence I needed to undertake the task of writing this book; my birth father's strong belief in the importance of helping most anyone in need led to my choosing this topic; and my stepfather's courage to deal with his own co-dependent behavior bolstered me during those difficult moments when researching this book unearthed more about my own problems than I believed, at first, I could bear.

Parents
Who Help
Their Children
Overcome
Drugs

To Parents Who Want to Help Their Children Overcome Drugs

I wrote this book in part because I wanted to help others and in part because I wanted to help myself. For years I had known of my younger sister's struggles with drugs, yet for years I had been unable to accept the fact that she was a substance abuser, that she really needed treatment, and that my reluctance to face the truth contributed in some significant ways to her addictive behavior.

The 10½-year difference in our ages had on many occasions put me in the position of acting as my sister's surrogate parent. I changed her diapers, warmed bottles and baby food, and slept without moving for hours with my infant sister cradled securely in my arms. When as a teenager she had difficulties getting along with our mother after our father's death and mother's remarriage, I even took on the responsibility of supporting her during some of her time as a college student. When she left the campus for holiday vacations, she stayed with me in Washington, D.C., not with our mother and stepfather in Los Angeles.

Given that history, one would think that at the very least I would have recognized that my sister was in some type of trouble when her college grades started to plummet inexplicably and when, years later, she was unable to pay her bills and could not provide plausible explanations of what had happened to her money. But I didn't recognize the signs because I opted to keep my head in the sand. In

1

retrospect, I simply didn't want to know that she had been using drugs for a number of years, starting with marijuana at 14 or 15 and ending with crack cocaine while pregnant during her mid-twenties.

These days, my sister is on the road to recovery, and so am I. We have both learned some important lessons, including the fact that her addictive personality was only one side of the coin. The way I related to her problem of substance abuse reflected a pattern of behavior on my part that was equally unhealthy. I was a co-dependent person whose own pathology of controlling and rescuing was triggered by my sister's pathology of manipulating in order to avoid responsibility for her chemical addiction.

My sister and I have also learned to accept that we are human, that we are imperfect, and that it is possible to carve out a constructive life despite our flaws and, most important, despite our mistakes. Through my participation in this book I have spoken to parents, their substance-abusing children, and drug-abuse professionals from all over the United States, and virtually every person I met reinforced that same lesson.

I am a writer, a sister, and a surrogate parent of sorts who has traveled the road on which you are about to embark. What I can say to you is this: Though the environment faced by parents who help their children overcome drugs is rife with challenges, it is also rife with opportunities for recovery. So, take heart in the book's underlying theme: A healthy family need not be perfect, only committed and courageous enough to work toward change.

How to Use
This Book

This book has been organized to help parents move themselves and their family members through a process of healing that comprises a number of phases. To that end, the six chapters in this book represent clearly delineated stages, from denial to eventual recovery. Each chapter begins with descriptions of my personal experiences as a sibling and surrogate parent trying to help my younger sister during her struggle with substance abuse. Each chapter ends with a case study of a family who has a similar story to tell. In between are straightforward and realistic explanations of what is required of families who want to help their children overcome drugs.

Chapter One, "Good Looks Are Deceiving," examines how easy it was for my family—and is for families in general—to engage in self-deception: While we clung to our pristine image, my sister was developing a heavy habit of using drugs. Chapter Two, "Co-dependency—On Being Addicted to the Addict," describes the role parents unwittingly play in "enabling" their child to use drugs when they make excuses or rescue their offspring from the harsh consequences associated with chemical addiction. Chapter Two also points out that this compulsion of some parents to go to extremes to "get things back to normal" constitutes a behavioral pattern as unhealthy as their child's substance abuse.

Chapters Three and Four—"Hanging Tough" and "Raising the Bottom, or Hanging Tough Phase II"—deal with the necessary lines parents must draw when their chemically addicted child repeatedly disregards the family's and society's rules. Chapter Five, "Treatment Options," presents the range of healing options available. The last chapter, "Letting Go," provides a more tolerant perspective of what constitutes success and recovery. There are also three appendixes: (A) a description of each state's policies concerning private health insurance coverage for services that help treat substance abusers, (B) a state-by-state list of treatment centers and support groups, and (C) a list of references and suggested readings.

The six case studies represent families with children, ages 14 to 22, who are either in the process of recovery or who have completed one or more treatment programs. These testifiers hail from cities throughout the United States, though most of the children have in common the fact that they spent time at Spring Creek Community, a therapeutic boarding school in Thompson Falls, Montana. The headmaster, Steven W. Cawdrey, was especially helpful in enlisting the cooperation of families whom he believed would willingly discuss the circumstances that led to their children's enrollment at his school.

Still, there were times when one or the other parent he referred refused to speak. There were instances when both parents wanted to share their experiences but the child did not want to talk about what had happened. A number of the parents and children had therapists or drug-abuse counselors who were willing to report on why they believed the families were in trouble. Of those parents, young people, and drug-abuse professionals who agreed to participate in the project, most requested their names be changed for anonymity. The stories they tell, though, are real, poignant, and frequently tough. You may cringe, cry, or chuckle at moments when you read the straight talk from these parents, their children, and the experts they asked for help.

With every case study, you will hear from the following family members in the order cited: mother, father, child in trouble, and sibling. I did very little editing and summarizing. For the most part, I transcribed the interviews and reported them as they were expressed to me. Given the way I decided to handle the material, there are inconsistencies, at times. For example, a father's depiction of a particular incident may not jibe with his daughter's version of what happened or his wife's interpretation of the same event. Moreover, the family therapist might provide yet another point of departure. Still, I made no attempt to get the parties to tell the same story the same way. I asked questions; I listened.

Because of this method, the case studies remind me of the classic Japanese saga, *Rashomon,* which concerns the difficulty of pinning down the truth. In that story, a tragic event is related through the eyes of several characters; however, each person's tale significantly changes the initial picture of what happened. Consequently, *Rashomon* is not one tale. Instead, it contains as many tales as there are characters. The result: Your sympathies are swayed by each recounting of the story. Similarly, as I interviewed family members and therapists for the case histories, my perspective invariably was altered as I heard the many points of view.

In the beginning, it was not unusual for me to silently support a particular family member who later fell out of favor once I heard what someone else had to say. With time, though, the multidimensional nature of the case studies led to an ever-emerging awareness of the complex issues faced by these families, thereby helping me to understand that there are no good guys or bad guys in these situations. Personally, that insight was significant, especially when I finally figured out that it applied as well to my mistakes and my family's experiences as to anyone else's.

This book may not be a quick read, since by definition *Parents Who Help Their Children Overcome Drugs* must cover some pretty rough terrain. Therefore, don't be surprised if some chapters are more difficult to read than others because they hit home uncomfortably. If that is your experience, it's okay to temporarily skip those sections to keep moving through the material, as long as you promise yourself to go back at some point and read what you have missed. Be patient with yourself and try to accept the fact that you and your family are involved in a healing process that will take time.

❧ *1* ❧

Good Looks Are Deceiving

I was raised in what could be labeled a dysfunctional family. My father was an alcoholic, a gambler, and, on occasion, a wife beater. There were times when my mother, under stress, drank too much. Yet we were middle class by virtue of my parents' occupations: Father drove a truck for the Post Office, and Mother was a schoolteacher. We were also middle class by virtue of the image the family steadfastly presented to the local community.

We lived in a nice, well-furnished house, dressed in the latest fashions, and had an abundance of toys. However, our good looks were deceiving. As in many families, what the public observed did not quite jibe with the day-to-day reality of our household. It was not unusual, for example, for us children to return home from school and find our father and his friends engaged in a drunken brawl. Our doorbell rang at all hours of the day and night with loan sharks demanding to know why Father had not paid his debts.

We grew up—my sister, brother, and myself—admonished to keep the family secrets. We found other ways, though, to act out what troubled us. To get out of the house and away from my parents, I married very young and soon had a child; my brother, who started high school enrolled in classes for exceptional students, eventually had trouble even with less challenging academic assignments; my sister soon began using drugs.

My parents' response to our individual rebellions varied. They pressured and at times punished me for my relationships with boys. They prodded my brother to improve his grades. However, my mother's typically aggressive posture did not hold up when it came to dealing with my sister's frequent use of marijuana by the time she was 15. Instead of trying to prevent it, my mother merely lamented it. The warrior on most every other front, my mother seemed helpless in the face of this unfamiliar challenge.

I did not understand the significance of what was happening to my sister; years later, I chose not to understand. My brother, the baby of the family, watched from the sidelines. My father was concerned but said nothing to my sister and little to anyone else. So the family continued to put forth its best possible face, despite our internal paralysis and inability to respond to my sister's SOS.

What I have learned in the years since is that many families, like individual people, have both public and private personas. The public persona attempts to provide an image of familial bliss or perfection. The private persona, on the other hand, reflects the authentic family dynamic, warts and all. If the private persona differs significantly from what the public is permitted to see, pressure is placed on both parents and children to maintain a false front. With time, it is inevitable that something or someone will buckle as rebellion sets in.

My sister's drug problem presented a familial blemish that would not go away. Her drug problem also represented a fissure in the family's facade. According to my sister, her use of drugs and her rebellion were fueled, at least in part, by a belief that our mother was trying to force her to be something she did not want to be. Despite good grades and high test scores, for example, my sister had no strong desire to attend college but enrolled in order to comply with our mother's expectations. Her college career lasted less than two years. Drugs and her disinterest played a role in her departure.

Clearly, my sister's behavior conflicted with the family's public persona. We were confused by the way she acted out her hostility. In retrospect, I also think we were afraid of what her acting out symbolized, what it might imply about the family's behavior. So it was easier, at least for a short time, for the family to hide behind a well-polished and well-rehearsed veneer of activity rather than to take the difficult step of admitting imperfection and then accepting the challenge to go public with my sister's problem by seeking outside help.

Ironically, mental health specialists would note that my sister's addiction could have served a very healthy function for the family had we mustered the courage to confront the problem. According to the experts, the "deviant" behavior of the child addict is frequently the stimulus that makes parents face and then accept that there is something out of line, something out of sync, with the family unit. In essence, the family is dysfunctional in some way. This type of confrontation is not a pleasant task for most parents. My family did not practice what I now preach. But, if there is a moral to this tale, it is that in the long run the challenge to change behavioral patterns, though at times uncomfortable, is a most worthwhile effort to undertake. Indeed, not to do so can be costly: No less than the good health and solid future of your child and, ultimately, your family are at stake.

THIS BOOK CAN HELP
ANY ADDICTIVE PERSONALITY

You are reading *Parents Who Help Their Children Overcome Drugs* because you either suspect or know that at least one of your children is using drugs. My sister abused marijuana and crack cocaine. Your son or daughter may have similar addictions or may be abusing a different combination of drugs. The particular drugs do not matter, in terms of how this book can be of use to you, because *Parents Who Help Their Children Overcome Drugs* will take you through a recovery process that views all substance-abusing youngsters as addictive personalities. Co-dependent family members, who adapt their behavior to accommodate the disruptions caused by the child's chemical addiction, are also considered addictive personalities. Family counselor Kathy Capell-Sowder of Dayton, Ohio, explains: "While it is commonly accepted that addiction to alcohol and drugs exists, it is less commonly understood that the person involved in a primary love relationship with someone addicted frequently displays symptoms of addiction himself in the ways that he relates to the relationship." This description of co-dependency applies as well to parents who are grappling with children who are abusing drugs. Thus, if you are a co-dependent parent this book will assist you in getting a handle on your own addictive behavior so as to minimize its effect on your troubled child.

Moreover, the book will direct you and your family

along a path that can lead to recovery. Although you will have to mobilize the courage to work for what you want, be patient with yourself and give yourself credit. After all, by having picked up this book you have already demonstrated a willingness to begin a most important journey.

THE FOUR KEY ISSUES

Parents Who Help Their Children Overcome Drugs is centered around four key issues: (1) Parents need to understand and accept the complex role they play in the lives of their substance-abusing children. (2) Parents need to learn how to help their children overcome drugs and how *not* to help. (3) Parents need to learn when it's okay to be selfish. (4) Parents need to understand the role faith plays in the recovery process.

At times these issues will overlap, because the problems under examination are interconnected. You will learn, for example, that your child's addiction is a function of your family's pathology as well as a factor in the negative dynamics your family displays (see Chapter Two, "Co-dependency—On Being Addicted to the Addict," and Chapter Three, "Hanging Tough"). My parents' dysfunctional behavior—Father's gambling and Mother's dictatorial dominance, for instance—certainly played some role in shaping the lives of my sister, brother, and myself. My sister acted out by using drugs; my brother acted out by doing poorly in school; I acted out by marrying early and by becoming a compulsive spender. On the other hand, our acts of rebellion reflected dysfunctional behavior that worked against healthy family interaction. Our antics added to the overall familial tension, which, in turn, sent my father dashing to the racetrack and led to my mother's further entrenchment into an authoritarian role: Since we were misbehaving, she felt she needed to run an even tighter ship. So, although the chapters are structured to cover separate topics, in truth, each subject is fundamentally connected to the others.

THE COMPLEX ROLE PARENTS PLAY

Admittedly, it's tough being a parent. Universities do not ordinarily provide courses in surefire techniques for successfully raising a family. The label "parent" is, by definition, complex: A mother and father are also a wife and husband and must struggle with the demands common to both roles. It is not easy being an authority figure for your children when you are a human being with foibles just like any other.

Still, there is no getting around the fact that when a person who happens to be a parent falters, the child often pays the price. When a parent develops a drinking problem, for example, behavioral patterns of broken promises and dishonesty undermine the child's confidence in the alcoholic parent and can lead to confusion, lethargy, and depression on the part of the child. Such feelings, in turn, can provoke the child to experiment with drugs in order to quell the discomfort associated with the parent's addiction to alcohol.

No family is perfect. Parents have to expect that they will make mistakes, albeit that is not an easy concept to accept. This book, through its narrative and case studies, will attempt to make that acknowledgment easier by helping you to understand the level of complexity associated with the role you as a parent play in your child's struggle with drugs. We will examine provocative questions: Is there such a thing as an addictive personality that describes your behavior as a non-drug user in terms that are similar to the behavior of your substance-abusing child? Did your bad habits contribute to your child's drug problem, or did your child's drug problem contribute to your current state of confusion and despair? Such questions are answered to some extent in this chapter and to a much larger degree in Chapter Two.

To help your child overcome drugs, another tough issue you will have to come to grips with is how to move beyond many forms of denial. For example, drug-abuse experts say that parents frequently write off the first indications of teenage drug use as "just a stage" of adolescent development. Indeed, in their book, *Loosening the Grip: A Handbook of Alcohol Information*, Jean Kinney and Gwen Leaton state that youthful alcohol abusers have been known to go as long as six years without being diagnosed.

No doubt it's hard to accept that a child, your child, is using drugs, but the truth is that the first step toward recovery—your child's, your own, and your family's—takes place when you decide to face facts, a topic that is discussed later in this chapter. Most of you who are reading *Parents Who Help Their Children Overcome Drugs* have already come this far and, thus, are ready for the next stage: learning how you can genuinely help your child.

DON'T ENABLE:
HOW TO HELP AND HOW *NOT* TO HELP

Learning how to help your child and how not to help your child is not as easy as it sounds, as demonstrated in Chapters Two on co-dependency, Four, "Raising the Bottom, or Hanging Tough Phase II," and Five, "Treatment Options." These chapters describe how parents fall into a pattern of behavior called enabling that actually works against a child's recovery process. Parents are considered enablers when they continue to rescue their children from the negative consequences of their drug-related actions.

Enablers are parents who routinely make excuses to school authorities for truant or disruptive behavior without knowing where their children actually were or what really happened. Enablers are parents who bear the expense of lawyers to help their child "beat" legal charges. Enablers are also parents who pretend that the valuables their child steals from the home to pay for drugs are simply items misplaced. Enablers consistently provide their children with "loans" that they never pay back and that go to purchase drugs.

Parents who enable are preventing their children from being connected to the consequences of their actions. By so doing, the parent is helping to undermine the child's confidence by implying that the child cannot handle her own affairs and by depriving the child of the opportunity to develop problem-solving skills. Often, the result is that the child's troublesome behavior escalates to a level that defies rescue and that carries an even stiffer price than earlier spates of wrongdoing. In truth, when you do not enable, you are treating your child with respect by displaying faith in his competence to get along in life. Treating yourself with respect is also important and sometimes requires that you display a benign form of selfishness.

IT'S OKAY TO BE SELFISH

It is possible to help your child overcome drugs and take care of yourself at the same time. Indeed, the narrative found in Chapter Three, "Hanging Tough," and in Chapter Four, "Raising the Bottom, or Hanging Tough Phase II," explains why it is sometimes necessary for you to learn

how to become selfish in order to lead your child successfully through the recovery process. There may come a time
when ensuring your own well-being will require that you
allow your substance-abusing child to hit bottom. Or there
may come a time when you find that you have to declare
your household a drug-free zone, where even cigarettes are
thought of as contraband, and you must insist that family
members who cannot abide by these rules must leave.
Chapters Three and Four make a strong case that being the
"bad guy" in the short term can really make you the good
guy over the long haul, because insisting on a healthy environment for yourself helps all concerned. Being tough,
however, requires strength and something less tangible but
even more powerful: faith.

HAVING THE FAITH TO LET GO

Finally, parents who help their children overcome drugs
have to learn how to have faith in themselves and in their
children's eventual recovery. In essence, you have to develop faith in your sincere efforts to help your child and
know that such efforts will provide a foundation of sorts
that will carry the young person for many years to come.
Chapter Six, "Letting Go," examines the topic of faith
through the testimony of parents of children with drug
problems.

FACING FACTS

Recovery, then, begins with acceptance that a drug problem does in fact exist. Parents are not the only family members who have difficulty moving beyond the appearance
of good looks in order to face facts about what is really

happening. It may be difficult for you to get a handle on what's ailing your adolescent, for example, because of your child's instinct to deny the existence of a substance-abuse problem. Some young people, like some adults, are quite skilled at hiding their addictions.

On the other hand, your child may be unaware of her own problem with drug abuse. Los Angeles-based psychiatrist and drug counselor Loren Woodson explains, "Often teenagers themselves don't realize that their drug problem is in fact a problem." Drugs are often part of a whole constellation of problems associated with young people. For example, it might be difficult at times to determine whether abnormal behavior is caused by learning disabilities, a dysfunctional family, or drugs.

Still, you have picked up this book for a reason. Probably that reason is your concern about having noticed at least several of the following behaviors—as listed in Kinney and Leaton's *Loosening the Grip*—that lead you to believe your child is using drugs:

The emergence of secretive or isolated behavior

A significant change in personal grooming

A significant change in health, such as repeated bouts with the flu, the emergence of apparent allergic symptoms, or chronic cough or chest pains

A sudden and inexplicable drop in grades

Possession of unexplained and large sums of money, or unexplained monetary losses

The emergence of new associates to the exclusion of former close friends

Emerging problems with short-term memory

Frequent accidents

Blocks of time not accounted for

A sudden change in schedule; for example, not returning home from school at the usual time

Physical or verbal abuse of younger siblings

Unexplained mood swings

A sudden decreased interest in previously favored activities such as sports and hobbies

A sudden change in personality, demonstrating feelings of loneliness, paranoia, and depression

A sudden disappearance of possessions from the home

The discovery of drug materials and equipment among a child's belongings

Beyond assisting you in establishing that a problem with substance abuse exists in your family, *Parents Who Help Their Children Overcome Drugs* will help you to better understand your youthful drug abuser. First, don't forget how hard it is to move through adolescence. Becoming an adult is a process that involves a great deal of stress under the best of circumstances. If there is a dysfunctional element in the family already, such as an alcoholic parent, or if family members have developed the habit of not talking to each other (like that reported in Marie Brenner's *House of Dreams*, a book about the infamous Bingham family of St. Louis, whose members wrote memos to communicate), the process of growing up is even more difficult.

In a lot of cases, substance abuse is the adolescent's response to the emotional hardships encountered while trying to complete the four fundamental tasks that comprise a young person's developmental process. Kinney and Leaton describe these tasks in *Loosening the Grip*. The first task involves accepting our biological role as males and females or, more to the point, as men and women. In some circles, drug use and abuse is part of that rite of passage. Drugs can come into play, for instance, as a sort of theatrical prop—a marijuana stick dangling from a young boy's mouth, or a teenage girl leaning forward to request a light from her youthful male counterpart, supports an image of male machismo and female sophistication and seduction.

When your child begins to identify with his or her gender, it also opens up the possibility of sexual intimacy—a threatening activity at best—and brings forward the second task: learning how to be comfortable with the opposite sex. Often young people use drugs to cope with feelings of vulnerability provoked by experimentations in the sexual realm.

The struggle to attain independence is yet another developmental baptism by fire required of your child. This task, which includes going head-to-head with parents, learning how to set limits for oneself, and developing the characteristics of a healthy and prosperous adult, is an especially difficult one for young people. During this period, your child's use of drugs tests limits and rules imposed by you, the parent. The message in Chapter Three, "Hanging Tough," speaks to the hard line you may be forced to take if you are faced with these circumstances.

As your adolescent approaches his early twenties, he must face the fourth task, which is to decide on some type of occupational identity. This phase is often marked by many false starts and thus "failures," as viewed by the adolescent. The great pressure associated with the need to succeed and the desire to break familial ties and move on can lead to heavy drug abuse.

What these four developmental stages do not explain is why, though every child experiences some of the discomfort connected with the completion of these tasks, not every child deals with it by using drugs. I experimented with some drugs as a child and as an adult, but for some reason I chose not to act out my rebellion by becoming a substance abuser. My sister, however, took a different route. You may have one child who uses drugs and two children who do not. Why that happens is not known, though some drug-abuse experts speculate that there may be a genetic predisposition for substance abuse and compulsive behavior that surfaces in one child and not in another of the same family.

What we do know, which parents need to face, is this. Becoming an adult is generally a pretty tough process to move through, and some young people try to cope by succumbing to drugs. Chapter Two, "Co-dependency—On Being Addicted to the Addict," discusses more thoroughly how parents can prepare their children to successfully handle the stresses and strains that are a part of this natural developmental process.

FROM HOPELESSNESS
TO HELP IN THREE STAGES

As a parent you try your best to fulfill your responsibility for the loving guidance of your child. Still, you are not perfect, as your child is not perfect. Try to keep that in mind as you turn the pages of this book and move from a position of helplessness to knowledge that there are things you can do to help your child.

The following three-stage scenario broadly describes the progression that ordinarily takes place within a dysfunctional family made more dysfunctional by having to cope with a young drug abuser. Not all families move through each stage. Some families get stuck in the first or second stages. Others experience all three stages only to fall prey again to the same behavioral patterns that fed the dysfunction in the first place. The bottom line is that the pathology between your drug-using child and the role you have played in your child's life cuts both ways. Still, just as you and your child share the "ailment," you and your child can recover by understanding the process that you both are going through and by working together to overcome the problems related to substance abuse and co-dependency.

EARLY STAGE: "SOLVING" THE PROBLEM

As a child's experimentation with drugs becomes an addiction, a parent's awareness typically moves from an all-encompassing denial that nothing bad is really happening, to a modified denial that seeks to establish a new set of standards for what is the norm. You make excuses to explain deviations in your child's pattern of behavior, and you describe gross deviations as isolated incidents, nothing to worry about.

In time, however, even the most blind parental eye comes to recognize that the child is in trouble. At that time, the parent makes an attempt to "solve" the drug-abuse problem by protecting the family and the dysfunctional member from external encroachment and ridicule. You may cover up for the substance abuser by making excuses to school authorities for truancy, for example, or by lying to other family members and friends about what is really going on. Unfortunately, such enabling tactics allow the child's behavior to continue unchecked, supporting rather than eradicating the symptoms of drug abuse. Enabling prevents the abuser from experiencing the pain and disruption that would signal there is something wrong in her life.

Enabling also prevents the family from facing its overall problems.

MIDDLE STAGE: ADAPTING TO ADDICTION

Normal efforts to eliminate the problem simply do not work. As the situation worsens with the substance-abusing child, the family's level of frustration and sense of failure increase as well. Still, during this period families tend to try even harder to help, although their efforts have not worked and will not work. Such families feed their own frustration by believing that the reason their children remain in trouble has something to do with the parents not making enough effort. So they try harder by literally taking on the responsibilities of the adolescent drug abuser, such as doing homework that has not been completed or paying for unpaid parking tickets, lost school books, or damaged cars.

CHRONIC STAGE: SINKING INTO CHAOS

At this stage the family has sincerely tried everything it knows to help the substance-abusing child and has failed, because virtually all of the family's attempts can be classified as enabling activities. Guilt, despair, and chaos are most often the outward expressions of that sense of failure. The family no longer believes in its ability to solve the problem. The only recourse is to seek outside help.

Though I have painted this progression in bleak terms, at every stage the opportunity for recovery exists for both the family and the affected child. As ensuing chapters and case studies will demonstrate, parents can indeed learn how to challenge and change old patterns of destructive behavior; adolescent drug abusers can also learn how to challenge and change their behavior patterns in a constructive and healthy manner. So, how do parents start to help their children overcome drugs? They can begin by turning the pages of this book slowly and by paying careful attention to the tales shared by parents, and sometimes the young abusers themselves, who have traveled the same road on which they are about to embark. The following case study provides one such opportunity to learn about the process of recovery.

On the face of it, this family is deceptively good-looking, a prototypical middle-class, suburban household: The husband is the primary wage earner, the wife has been a housewife during most of the marriage, and the three off-spring are attractive children who, according to the mother, "have never really wanted for anything." Yet the oldest child has been using marijuana and cocaine for a number of years, though he is only 20.

CASE STUDY:
SHARON, JOHN, AND AARON

Sharon's voice quavers at times when she talks about her 20-year-old son, Aaron. Sharon, 44, describes the last seven years of her life as "living in hell" because of what she has experienced while trying to cope with her son's drug habit. A housewife, Sharon has been supported financially by her husband, John, for most of the 23 years they have been married. However, she feels she has not received emotional backup from John in dealing with Aaron's drug problems.

John, 45, takes a stoic and more hard-line approach when he discusses Aaron's recent past, although there are signs that he worries, as does Sharon, about what will become of Aaron. "The wife and I deal with things differently. I wasn't asleep when Aaron was doing some of the things he was doing. She just thinks I was sleeping."

In addition to Aaron, Sharon and John have two daughters—Monique, 22, and Nicole, 19. This is a home-owning, middle-class family living in a suburban section of Los Angeles that was once farmland. Today, many of the neighborhood streets are populated by teenage dope dealers, who make most of their money through the sale of cocaine. Sharon and John know a lot about this life because of John's occupation—he heads a program that finds jobs for economically disadvantaged young people—and because their son spent many a night on these streets selling crack cocaine in order to support his own habit.

SHARON

Sharon looks tired as she explains that the past seven years have produced nightmare experiences. She describes a scene where Aaron was in the middle of the street and a woman, screaming that Aaron had sold her some "bunk" dope and she wanted her money back, held a knife to his neck. On another occasion, Sharon was in her kitchen cooking when Aaron, closely followed by a knife-wielding youngster, burst into the back door and led a chase through the first floor of the family's home.

According to Sharon, these experiences only begin to tell of the pain, uncertainty, and worry that started when Aaron was only 13. At that time, in 1981, Sharon received a call from her husband reporting that Aaron had been caught using marijuana with friends. She was dismayed by the news, Sharon says, but she had "expected that this day would come."

Over the years, their neighborhood had changed, and

Sharon was concerned. Some of the local children who were Aaron's age had older brothers and sisters in jail. "Aaron's best friend's brother had been in jail. And Aaron was very attached to this kid because Aaron didn't have a brother," she explains. She wanted to get Aaron out of the neighborhood—to enroll him in a private school or to uproot the entire family and move. But, she reports, with a note of bitterness in her voice, "John said no." Her husband's rationale was that their family should stay and become the "leaders of the community. It seems to me that John wants us [the family] to be community leaders at any cost."

Her husband was motivated to remain in the community because of the way he was raised. "John's family was the most well-off family of the local community. John had many more opportunities and economic advantages than the other kids in the neighborhood, and he was resented for having so much more and ridiculed for being made by his parents to go to music classes and things like that." The result, Sharon points out, is that John has rebelled against his upbringing in a number of ways. He uses colloquial language, for example, and he refuses to move away from the community in which they currently live.

So they stayed, and by the time Aaron was 16 he had been introduced to cocaine. Sharon explains: "One of Aaron's friends was dating a woman about eight years his senior. This girlfriend would invite the neighborhood boys over and supply them with marijuana cigarettes laced with a crystal-type substance that I later found out was crack cocaine. If I had known the danger of it, I would have put my foot down. I would have really watched Aaron's every movement. But, at the time, I didn't know that some people can get addicted to crack almost immediately."

During this period, Aaron, a child who had been

placed in classes for the mentally gifted while in elementary school, was arrested for the first time. He was caught stealing expensive bicycles from racks at the local college, delivering the contraband to a man in the neighborhood who paid Aaron and his buddies $20 for their efforts. Sharon was puzzled by the phone call from the police station. "We're not rich or anything, but my kids were not deprived," she says, so why would Aaron need to steal? Sharon and John later discovered that Aaron's cocaine habit was what motivated him to steal, including objects that belonged to members of the household. However, it took another example of abnormal behavior before Sharon and John really understood that their son was addicted to cocaine and how that addiction was damaging his life.

After that first arrest, things rapidly went from bad to worse. "He started ditching school at around the same time he started stealing, and he had never been rebellious at school. Then, besides missing his classes, Aaron started coming home later and later. He also started coming home with a lot of money in his pockets." Soon the family heard rumors that their son was spending his evenings selling drugs on one of the local streets. The tales were confirmed one day when a man in his mid-thirties, who had served time for murder and was known as a recruiter of children to sell drugs, knocked on the door looking for Aaron. Sharon says, "When we demanded to know what this guy wanted with Aaron, he told us, 'I put money in Aaron's pocket.'" Aaron's explanation: "I've made some deliveries for him."

From that moment forward, Sharon reports, her nightmare odyssey began. "I went to the street and actually saw Aaron hailing cars down to sell drugs. All of this started in 1985, a few months before his seventeenth birthday. So every night his sisters and I would get in the family truck and zoom down this street and make Aaron come home. He would hide in the bushes or behind a tree to avoid us. After a while, he was able to recognize the truck by its missing headlight, so I starting driving down the street with the lights out on the truck in order to fool him. Once I even brought a baseball bat with me to use as a threat to make sure Aaron got in the truck to go home. Every night the girls and I went after him. And we never came home without him.

"It got so that I was a nervous wreck, because I was keeping the same hours as Aaron. I was out all night most every night. My oldest daughter also suffered because she was the one who went with me most of the time. My husband slept through it all." Sharon kept trying, because she couldn't give up on her son. In addition, "A few times he told me he couldn't help it, that he was hooked on the drugs and couldn't help himself."

A year after Aaron's initial involvement with crack, he was in a near-fatal automobile accident. Because he had traces of cocaine in his blood, the medication that could save his life wasn't working as well as it should have. He did recover, and for about the first 30 days after his return from the hospital, "Aaron was a model son at first. He was clean of dope. He helped around the house. He was sweet. He was the son that he used to be. When he got his insurance settlement from the accident he was very generous and started buying neighborhood people presents.

"Around that time someone in the neighborhood decided to reintroduce Aaron to crack to get more money from him. And this time when Aaron became addicted, he was completely out of control. He would put his fist through walls when he didn't get what he wanted, or scream and holler when things didn't go his way." It didn't take Aaron long to run through his insurance settlement, which sent him back into the streets to obtain the money to support his drug habit.

This time, Aaron's drug-dealing activities took place in the front yard of the home. "I asked him not to run the streets because of what had happened to him as a result of the car accident," Sharon says, "so he starting selling cocaine in front of the house. Cars would drive up at all hours of the night. I would stand out front and take license plate numbers and threaten to turn the buyers in to the police. I would argue with the guys who were standing in my front yard purchasing the dope. John stayed in bed. I really believe that if a man, my husband, had been outside doing what I was doing, he could have put a stop to the dope traffic. But my efforts didn't keep the thugs away."

Eventually, Aaron sold cocaine to an undercover police officer and was arrested. He was released to enter a drug treatment center. Aaron lasted a few days in one treatment facility, a month in another, and finally settled in a long-term (six to nine months) residential treatment program that appears to be a good fit. Sharon's never-say-die attitude about her son's drug problems was strengthened by thoughts she had had after Aaron's close bout with death: "After the accident I used to think, 'Is Aaron going to die without having known what it felt like to live a full and clean life?' I began to think, 'If he were dead, how would I help some other kid in a position similar to Aaron's before his death?' And then whatever ideas I came up with, I would transfer the thoughts to Aaron by pointing out to myself that he was still alive.

"Every time Aaron was in trouble, everyone wanted us to use 'tough love' tactics. Everyone wanted Aaron put out into the streets, including my husband, but I wouldn't let John do that, even though sometimes I thought about it. Drug dealers *want* kids to be put out on the streets.

Besides, I believed I should keep trying because you've never tried everything. Now Aaron thanks me for not giving up on him."

JOHN

"It ain't so much where you live, but how you live where you live," says John, who has a bachelor of arts degree in behavioral science, in explaining why he refused to allow the family to leave the area even after it became difficult to pull Aaron away from a local crowd that used and sold drugs. Unlike Sharon, John doesn't blame the neighborhood for their son's problems: "The neighborhood hoodlums didn't come out in front of the house except for what Aaron brought in front of the house. It ain't the neighborhood, it's what Aaron was doing in the neighborhood that was the problem." Besides, John adds, "I came from a background where I stayed in a house that I grew up in all of my life, so I don't like moving." John, Sharon, and the children have lived in the same house for 20 years.

"At first I didn't want to believe Aaron was on crack," John recalls. "But then our camera, tools, jewelry, anything that couldn't be nailed to the floor, was stolen from the home. Aaron was arrested for selling cocaine, he was convicted of armed robbery. . . . Sharon feels I don't have any confidence in Aaron. But it's just that I know what that cocaine can do to you and I believe that it takes a superperson to overcome this. I don't know that Aaron is a superperson. In fact, I don't know anyone who is a superperson."

These days, John thinks a lot about the impact Aaron's ordeal has had on himself, Sharon, and their two daughters. "I wasn't asleep when the old lady was out in the middle of the night chasing Aaron. You can't sleep during that kind of situation. But you can't stay up all night either, because you have to get up in the morning. What I had to deal with was, I was the only one working. Sharon spent so much time trying to handle Aaron's problem, she neglected everything and everyone else, including me."

On the other hand, he says, "Sharon was a punching bag. If she took Aaron's side, I got angry. If she took my side, Aaron got angry. I bet she wondered, 'If these are the two men in my life that love me, I don't need any enemies.' What I feel good about, though, was how the girls dealt with the problem. No matter how angry they were about having their personal belongings stolen by their brother, they always felt that they could get another necklace, but their brother had a problem." John does admit, however, that his oldest daughter still stays up most of the night from having spent so many evenings roaming the streets with her mother in search of her brother.

When asked what he thinks of Sharon's comment that the price paid for the family to stay in the community and maintain a position of leadership may have been too high, John says, "I think about that now and then." In a quieter voice, he adds, "Sometimes I wonder if she's right."

AARON

"All of my friends were doing it [using drugs], so I started doing it, too," explains 20-year-old Aaron, speaking during his second month at a long-term residential drug treatment center. Aaron is quick to point out, however, that peer-group pressure was only one of two reasons he started smoking marijuana at 14 or 15. The other reason: "I had a good time when I used drugs; I had fun."

Aaron's "good times" continued after he entered high school, when his substance abuse expanded to include alcohol. "There was a park near my high school where we would hang out and get high. I started ditching classes to drink beer and smoke marijuana." According to Aaron, his parents became alerted to the fact that something was wrong as his school attendance declined significantly. After a while he simply stopped going to school.

His parents had very different attitudes about what should be done. "My mother would say stuff like, 'Not my son. He's not using drugs.' Now my father, he knew what was going on and wanted to ground me, but my mother had the final say-so and wouldn't let him do anything to me." Meanwhile, Aaron's habit grew to include cocaine by the eleventh grade, when the older girlfriend of one of his buddies introduced him and other teenage boys to a marijuana stick laced with cocaine, which she called a primo.

Puffing on a primo produced a feeling unlike anything Aaron had previously experienced. "I got a rush from smoking it. I can't explain any better than that how good it felt. I just can't explain it." His addiction to primos sent him out into the streets in desperate search of money. Approximately five primos could be derived from one cocaine rock, and one rock at that time cost $25. To meet such expenses, he reports, "I had to start doing things to get my money together to pay for the four to six primos I was smoking a day. So I started snatching purses, stealing car radios, doing little things like that."

As he smoked more, his tolerance for primos increased and thus he needed to smoke even more to feel the rush. When he developed a $50-a-day habit, his criminal activities escalated to include breaking into homes and strong-armed robberies. Aaron's voice drops to a whisper as he explains what strong-armed robbery is: "It's when you beat up people and steal from them." When Aaron's consumption of primos reached the $400-a-day range, he turned to selling cocaine. He would pick up a sack filled with $500 worth of cocaine, which the supplier would provide on credit, providing Aaron returned $300 in sales within a certain time. The $200 profit margin was Aaron's cut for dealing dope.

Aaron traveled from street to street selling cocaine, changing locations only when a particular avenue became "hot" with police infestation. Eventually he was caught by the authorities but not, at first, for his drug activities. "I finally got popped by the police for a strong-armed robbery." Aaron and a few friends had decided to rob a woman. In the process of snatching her purse, one of the boys hit her, though Aaron says that it was not he. They got caught when the driver of their getaway car drove down a dead-end street, giving bystanders time to take down the license number. Later the same evening, a detective knocked on Aaron's door and he was arrested.

Three months later Aaron was in a near-fatal car accident. He and a friend had been getting high off cocaine all day and drinking. The accident occurred when his friend tried to drive onto a main highway, lost control of the car, and ran into a rail. Aaron flew out the back window. He was on the critical list for two months, in a coma for six weeks of that time. When he came out of the coma he was paralyzed from the neck down. He did regain his physical mobility in a few days, but it took longer for his memory to be restored—about a month.

"The doctors had told my mother that they didn't think I was going to make it. And if I did make it, they said I wouldn't remember anybody for at least eight years. But through the grace of God, everything started coming back. They had psychiatrists working with me and I was doing all of this work on computers and stuff." Computer puzzles and games were used to test how much of his capacity to remember remained. But, he adds, "Before they would release me from the hospital, I had a meeting with all the specialists and all the doctors and they told me, 'Aaron, we know you're an addict.' I looked at them like they were crazy. I said, 'What are you talking about?' I had forgotten all of this. So they told me that if I continued to use cocaine once I got out, I could probably have a relapse.

"My accident caused me to have a lot of swelling around the brain and they had to drain it. They said that cocaine is a drug that goes straight to the brain. And they said that that [using cocaine] could possibly cause the swelling to start again and that I might not be so fortunate the next time. So I got out of the hospital and I wasn't messing around with any drugs or drinking. Then I got my $50,000 settlement from the accident and I was doing good. But then one of my friends had this sick idea that we were going to become rich by selling cocaine. So I started back selling cocaine again and I was making a lot of money."

Along with his return to the streets to deal dope, Aaron began to drink and "smoke a little marijuana." He was not using cocaine at first. "But one of my so-called partners, who wasn't in the car with me selling the cocaine and who wasn't making all the money I was making, asked me if I wanted a Buddha Thai joint [an especially potent type of marijuana]. I said, 'Yeah,' and stuck it in my top pocket. Later on that night I went outside to smoke it, and I lit it up and I took a puff and I said, 'Damn, this don't taste like no Buddha Thai.' And then I smelled it and it smelled kind of good. Then I took a big hit and I blew it out and I said, 'Oh my God, this is a primo.'"

At that moment, Aaron got scared and threw the primo to the ground and ran into his home acting paranoid he says, because he didn't know what to do. "So I called up my girl and I told her I was going to come get her and then go get a motel room. Then I went and picked up a half-ounce of cocaine. When I got to the room I smoked up about half of that half-ounce and then I called my partner up, and we stayed there about a day and a half just smoking cocaine. My cocaine habit started back right then."

This time, Aaron had so much money from selling cocaine that he moved quickly to an expensive primo dependency. "When I first started [smoking primos] after I got out of the hospital, I was spending about $200 every now and then on cocaine. Then it started to be $200 just about every day. Then it was $200 or $300 every day. My father was aware of what was going on, so they stopped giving me my [settlement] money. But then I had to start selling drugs again because they weren't giving me my money. If I had a bad day and didn't earn much, I would still ask my father or my mother for some money, but they would say no. So I started stealing from home. I never used to steal from home, but, see, I'd bought a lot of gifts for them. So I said, 'Well, I bought you all of this stuff and you can't give me any money?' And they said, 'No, Aaron. We know what you're doing with it.' So I started stealing from home." When he couldn't generate enough funds from what he took from his family, Aaron returned to the streets with a vengeance.

"It got to the point where I was back on the streets selling dope every day. Then I hooked back up with my partner, and together we were totally smoked out. We were smoking $600 or $700 a day. After a while, I got tired of walking to other places to sell the cocaine, so we turned our street into a dope street. The police became aware of what we were doing. The neighbors became aware of what we were doing. My father was aware of what we were doing, and my mother finally came around to being aware of what we were doing."

Aaron's father told him he knew Aaron was an addict and asked if he wanted help to overcome his problem with drugs. "I said no. So my father said, 'Well, if you're going to do it [sell and use drugs], keep the shit away from my house.' So we would walk down the street and sell, but when it got late, I used to stand out in front of the house." Soon he was arrested for possession of cocaine with intent to sell. In exchange for doing some undercover work for the police department, Aaron got off with no time served and only two years' probation. The experience caused him to stop selling drugs in front of his home, but it did not cause him to stop smoking cocaine, although he did reduce his habit to "only about $75 a day."

This time, to support his addiction, Aaron and his friends started manufacturing phony cocaine, which they sold to unsuspecting clients as the real thing. "We started beating people out of their money. We would get some Monterey jack cheese and then leave it on the roof for about a week. Then we would cut it up and let the cheese rocks sit for a while in the oral gel that you put on your teeth. Then we would take the pieces out and let them dry out and get hard. When that happened, the cheese would look just like rocks of cocaine. One day I sold $400 worth of it. People would come back and I would deny that I had even sold them that, and by that time I would have real cocaine, so I would give them a little piece of mine, so they would end up buying some more. It was a crazy game."

Aaron has since discovered that his volatile life impacted his parents' life in an equally volatile way. "I found out in here [the residential treatment center] that they [parents] go through the same states of depressions that we do. My mother was to the point where she was asking herself, 'Why me? What did I do wrong? I thought I raised him right.' She got to the point where she just cut me off. She believed that I was going to do what I wanted to do, and all that she could do was pray for me."

Around this time, Aaron called his probation officer, after not having reported as required for about two months. The conversation was a sobering one: "My probation officer said, 'Sorry, buddy, I've turned you in. I made a recommendation that you go to the state penitentiary.' He said he was tired of seeing guys like me take advantage of their families. He felt that the only way for me to see the light was to do some time, some long time. So I panicked and told my mom. We were almost to the point where I was going to go to Canada and stay with some relatives up there, because I didn't want to go to the penitentiary.

"I talked to my father and he said, 'They're going to catch you anyway, you've got to come back sooner or later.' So I called my lawyer and he told me that the only thing I probably had going for me was if I got into a long-term [treatment] program, because usually if you get into a program they won't snatch you out to take you to jail. So I went to this one program up in Lancaster in the middle of the desert. But I was the youngest person there, everybody else was about thirty-five and up. So I really didn't fit in, I didn't feel comfortable. I called my mom and dad and told them that I was doing good, that I was praying and everything, then the next day I called them and told them that I was out of the program, that I couldn't take it. So my father picked me up and took me home. I had been clean about ten days, so I was looking better—the bags under my eyes had started to go away. The first day I was back my mom bought me all types of little things and I didn't mess with any drugs that day, I just hung around the house watching videos."

Trouble started the next day, however. As Aaron sat outside the house with his sisters, a former cocaine client drove up and waited to see if Aaron would serve him. "This guy was a guy who always spent like a hundred or more dollars. So I was thinking to myself, 'Should I do it?' I didn't know if I should because I had been clean. But I said, '———— it,' and I ran out to the car with him and I heard my sister screaming, 'Mommy, Mommy, Mommy!'

"So I went back and stood at the side of the house and I smoked a primo. Then I went inside the house and I saw my sister crying. Then I walked down the hallway and I saw my dad, who said, 'Go look and see what you've done to your mother.' And I thought, 'Damn, what did I do? What did I do?' So I went back there and she was just in a hysterical condition. She was crying and crying and she wouldn't talk to me. So I went into my room and I started crying. When I came out, my other sister said that she hated me; my father slammed me to the wall and told me that my mother had to go to the hospital because of what I had done to her. So I got this idea. I got my father's keys to his office where I knew he kept a gun. I got the gun, hopped into my car, and went to the nearest park. I was crying and everything, thinking, 'Why am I here? I just messed up my whole family. I'm the cause of all of these problems.' I decided to kill myself. I pulled the cock back, but the clip wasn't in the gun. So I thought to myself, 'Damn, there must really be a God.' "

Aaron returned home that evening to a calmer environment. He was able to talk to his mother, and the next day he entered the program he is in now. He has been clean ever since—at the time of this interview, approximately 120 days. It feels good, he says, for a number of reasons. "I want to stay clean now because I'm back to where I can talk to my father. He respects me now. He doesn't call me names and stuff. And my sisters like me. Well, they always liked me, but now I can see the love in everybody." These days, Aaron says that he has some goals he wants to achieve.

"I'm not a dumb person. I want to take some courses in public speaking, I want to get my high school diploma, and I want to work with my father."

POSTSCRIPT

According to his drug counselor, Barbara Green of the Pomona, California-based American Hospital, Aaron has come a long way in the two-and-a-half months he has been in this program. "The Aaron that's sitting across from me now is attempting to become humble, trusting, open-minded, and is in touch with himself and his feelings," she says. "The Aaron that I met when he first came into this program was a very angry, hostile, nontrusting individual."

Most of what Aaron has yet to achieve, Green says, centers around problems with his co-dependent family, especially his mother. "Aaron has walked through a lot of pain in his life already," Green notes, "but right now he has to find a way to feel like an accomplished person so that he can leave this program and become a productive member of society without relying on his mother as much as he does now. We call it detachment with love—that's what we're trying to help him with now."

Both Aaron and his mother are involved in multi-family therapy groups. It's turning out to be more difficult for his mother to detach than for Aaron, Green reports. "I thought it would be the other way around. But it's proving to be real tough on his mother." When Aaron first arrived and Green told him he needed to take a look at the co-dependency issue between himself and his mother, that he needed to break away, Aaron resisted mightily. "He was still in his bad-head stage and believed that all I wanted to do was make him stop loving his mom. But that wasn't it at all. I just wanted him to grow up."

Green considers it a good sign, then, that Aaron is talking more and more about how he wants to get to know his father better. This suggests Aaron is moving in the right direction, because his father is a "tough-love type of guy."

"To be honest with you," Green says, "Aaron is the one case that I thought I would have the most trouble with. What I think happened is that early on Aaron called one of his peers here a punk. That kind of language is unacceptable. So I give him a discipline, which is a learning experience. I gave him a topic to write about on respect and that's when the change happened here."

The day she gave Aaron that assignment, she recalls, he was very upset with her and the entire program. "His peers took him out into the back parking lot and walked him around and just let him vent his anger. At that time Aaron wanted to leave the program. His peers told him that staying in the program was what he needed to do; however, it was his decision. If he wanted to remain a sick person and not get better, that was his choice also."

Green offers the following thoughts as to why Aaron responded with such anger to a relatively mild reprimand: "I can only tell you what my gut tells me, and that is I think Aaron—who knew exactly what buttons to push around his mother, an enabler, to make her respond the way she did—was really angry with me for making him take a look at that behavior and angry with himself for having taken advantage of his mother's enabling behavior for so long."

At this point in the recovery process, Green gives Aaron a prognosis of "fair" in terms of overcoming his chemical dependencies. To that end, Green is working with Aaron to help him find a place to stay outside his home community, Pomona. "Aaron has already told me that he does not want to remain in Pomona, and I am helping him explore other possibilities, including going into the service—an idea his mother doesn't like. She wants him to return to the home. But we're working on her— that's why we have multifamily group therapy."

Aaron's mother still worries about what will happen when he gets out of the treatment program. But, she feels, "It's my duty as a parent to do everything I can to help Aaron, and to never, never, never give up." Aaron's father is also apprehensive about how Aaron will fare when he is released, but his thoughts focus more on what new rules should be established for Aaron to live by. Explains John: "He's never really had to work. My thing is, if you're going to live here [in the family home], you're going to have to live by my rules, and that includes getting a job. I love my son very much, but I want him to become his own man."

At a recent multifamily group therapy session, the parents were asked to write down what they really wanted to see change in their relationship with their substance-abusing child. Most of the parents, John explains, came up with statements such as they wanted to "improve communications." However uncomfortable it made him, John opted to make a more provocative comment. "This may sound selfish," he told the other parents, "but what I'd like is for my kids to become more independent, to start doing something on their own. I want some peace and quiet for myself, and I want some quality time with my wife."

John also admitted to the group that he still broods about some of the activities Aaron got involved in when he was using drugs. "There's a lot of hostility and anger in me about what he did. So it's going to take more than a couple of months of Aaron being in this program before I'm going to forget about what he put our family through."

Do Sharon and John need treatment in order to better deal with their son? Sharon has been labeled a co-dependent. Is John? Have Sharon and John enabled Aaron to live the drug-related lifestyle he led for so many years? Chapter Two, "Co-dependency—On Being Addicted to the Addict," sorts out the questions raised by the experiences of this couple.

❧ 2 ❧

Co-dependency
—On Being Addicted
to the Addict

For years I helped my sister use drugs by refusing to acknowledge that there was something wrong and by at times adapting my lifestyle, and consequently the rules that ordinarily governed my life, to her addictive behavior. My way was to simply not see, as had been our father's way as well.

Our parents separated when my sister was nearly 14 and I was 24 and away at college. My sister opted to live with my father, who worked the night shift. Her involvement with drugs began during that period: Most evenings, she left the house shortly after Father left for work.

She explains, "Dad and I never discussed where I was or what I did when he was at work. Dad may have surmised, Dad may have presumed, but Dad didn't *know* because he never asked." Part of the problem in communications stemmed from the fact that my mother and father were going through a bitter divorce and Father viewed my sister as a miniature of my mother.

According to my sister, "Dad saw more and more of

Mom in me. So he just resented me more and more. He never dealt with me on my own level, and Mom didn't deal with me at all, so I was alone. All I had were my friends." In an attempt to escape the unpleasantness of her life, she turned to drugs. "I liked getting high," she recalls, "but the high isn't what kept me doing it—it was the escape that went along with the process of getting high. I didn't have anyone, so that's what I was turned on to, the escape."

Soon my sister's nighttime activities began to interfere with her day. She became more and more lethargic. She slept during the day and often remained home from school. Though all signs pointed to drug or alcohol abuse, my father never pressed her for answers; he never asked what was causing her to change.

My turn came some years later when my sister, then 26, moved in with me. By then she was addicted to crack or rock cocaine. At best I can say I didn't know her problems were drug related, at least not initially. At worst I can say I suspected as much but really didn't want to know. Even now, I'm still not clear which is true, but I can admit these days that the way I adapted to her abnormal behavior allowed her addiction to flourish.

One of the first ways I covered for her was financially. Though she worked every day, she seldom seemed to have any money. In the beginning, I thought a lot about why that was so, but I eventually made excuses for her monetary shortages and paid the bills myself.

Another way I adapted to her addiction was to dutifully report to other family members and friends how well she was doing. I worked on the assumption that to tell the truth about my sister's personal affairs would somehow betray her, that what she did was her own business and should not be reported to others. Moreover, I played the same game with her as had my father years earlier: It was not until the very end of her stay with me that I even questioned her about her use of drugs. Like my father, I avoided asking the hard questions. In retrospect, I believe I did what I did because I had many of the same feelings that my sister reports having felt. In essence, had I discussed her "problem" with others as well as with her, I would have had to confront the fact that I was as out of control in my life as she was in hers, and that I felt as isolated and as helpless as she.

Not surprisingly, my behavior enabled my sister's behavior to become worse. It was not long before she could not catch up with her debts. Soon she was disappearing for days at a time, and when she did return home it was obvious that she was wide-eyed and "wired" from drugs.

Still, I did not request that she leave my home. Instead, I paid the bills and continued to provide her with a haven where she was guaranteed shelter, food, and unlimited use of a phone, and where no questions were asked. I resented her, however, and her attitude suggested she resented me. We barely spoke to each other. When she was home, she stayed sequestered in her bedroom most of the time. I begrudged her use of the telephone. I begrudged her trips to the refrigerator. In general, I begrudged her very presence. Yet I never said a word to her about my anger and frustration or about what I was finally beginning to suspect: My sister was an abuser of drugs.

Experts now consider such capitulation to an addict's behavior an illness in its own right. My behavior was typical of the co-dependent. I was addicted to my sister's addictive behavior. As defined by Sharon Wegscheider-Cruse, a California-based drug-abuse counselor, co-dependency "is a primary disease. . . . It is what happens to family members when they try to adapt to a sick family system that seeks to protect and enable the alcoholic [or drug-dependent person]. Each family member enters into this collusion in his own individual way."

As is always the case, my co-dependent behavior hurt myself as well as my sister. For example, I have since learned that I was motivated to "protect" my sister's image from family and friends in order to assume a position of control over my sister's life. By so doing, I hoped, on some unconscious level, that my sister would feel grateful and thus owe me allegiance. The point of this elaborate ruse of exercising control was that I needed to feel needed, even if to do so required my sister's emotional subjugation. Such co-dependent behavior on my part impaired my sister's already low self-esteem, since the message I sent to her was: You must be a bad person, because to upgrade your image I have to tell a bunch of lies.

So, as a co-dependent person, I fed on my sister's abnormal behavior. To some extent my sister fed just as heavily on my co-dependent responses to her drug-related actions. What we became, then, were two members of an unhealthy team who played the same destructive game over and over again.

Parents who want to help their children overcome drugs have to learn how to break that cycle. The chapters that follow cover how to accomplish this, bringing up such matters as "hanging tough"—learning when and how to draw the line—in addition to approaches to treatment options for parents and their troubled children.

PORTRAIT OF A CO-DEPENDENT

As a parent of a child who abuses drugs, you may already recognize yourself as a co-dependent personality. You have probably felt it your responsibility to maintain the family's equilibrium, knocked out of kilter by your child's chemical dependency. As a co-dependent, it's likely that you have tried to take on the responsibilities abandoned by your child, such as doing her neglected homework or paying for dented fenders caused by her driving under the influence of alcohol or drugs. Sometimes you've lied to protect your child, your family, and (not least) your psyche. Often you've vacillated from entirely accepting the "blame" for your child's chemical dependency to projecting the blame onto someone else or something else that will not or cannot refute the allegation. My father, for example, died when my sister was 16. It is much easier for my mother (and, I must admit, myself at times) to blame my father for many of the family's ills than to share in that blame.

According to Jael Greenleaf, president of Los Angeles-based Greenleaf & Associates, an organization that specializes in conducting workshops for adult children of alcoholics, additional co-dependent behaviors include:

An Inflated Sense of Self

By living your own life as well as taking over the day-to-day responsibilities abandoned by your drug-abusing child, you feel that you are a superhuman person. Yet because you are hoping to exact a price of emotional subservience from your child in return for your efforts to "save" her, the bionic image you maintain of yourself is tainted by the feeling of martyrdom.

Distrust of Your Child

Often, when faced with a child who is using drugs, parents naively believe that they have the power to personally and quickly make their child stop substance abuse, or they think that the child himself can stop on his own without help. The child may fuel that belief by promising time and time again that he has broken the habit, only to start up again. Children who feel compelled to offer such false promises have to lie about many other activities to hide the fact that they are still using drugs. Eventually, co-dependent parents learn to distrust their children.

A Tendency to Lie

Some co-dependent parents who learn to live with the lies their sons and daughters tell also begin to tell lies themselves to support what they want to believe about their children. Parents lie as well to "protect" their children from exposure. Whatever motivates the lie, being dishonest typically produces guilt in the parent and child, though they rarely acknowledge the guilt.

A Judgmental Attitude Toward Others

Co-dependent parents tend to find fault with children of other families, with their neighborhood, with their spouses, with most anything and anyone except themselves. They display this type of behavior in order to deflect attention from the so-called failure of their family, exemplified by a drug-abusing child. Severe and continual judgment of others that stems from a feeling of isolation further perpetuates that feeling.

Solitariness

Feeling helpless and unable to change their children's behavior often causes co-dependent parents to feel like failures and to feel ashamed of that perceived failure. So they withdraw and become antisocial. Sometimes they act out such behavior in a way that causes them to appear snobbish. They may start to shun longtime friends of the family, for example.

Depression

Feeling down-and-out is considered "the common cold of psychopathology." Basically, depression is fueled by loss. Co-dependent parents feel a loss of legitimate power over their troubled children. Parents who have made plans for the futures of their sons and daughters become frustrated and finally despondent as they watch their substance-abusing children slowly self-destruct.

Do you recognize yourself in this portrait of a co-dependent? I saw myself among these examples, and once I got over the shock, I began to take steps to redraw the portrait. You can use this information, as I did, to start a self-enlightenment process. Just reading the list of co-dependent behaviors helped me to become aware of the self-defeating ways I acted out my feelings of frustration, helplessness, and fear.

First, I made it a point to take note of my co-dependent reactions to family members and friends. I didn't try to alter my behavior in the beginning; I just tried to pay close attention so that I could understand what or who was more or less likely to trigger a co-dependent response from me. Later, I would imagine other ways I might have responded to the same circumstance. With time, I developed the courage to experiment with other, more healthy, behavioral approaches. Nowadays, I still slip into co-dependent patterns of behavior, but less frequently than before.

Thus, by redrawing your own portrait of co-dependency, you can gain more control over your life while becoming less manipulative of others. An added benefit of redrawing your portrait is that you will become less vulnerable to the manipulative behavior of your substance-abusing child. Indeed, as the next section points out, it is all too easy for parents of children who use drugs to fall victim to the addictive-personality syndrome, where mother, father, and child alike feed on each other's co-dependencies.

LOSING CONTROL/GAINING CONTROL

As your child becomes more and more dependent on drugs, she will play out a downward spiral that can end with her having lost control of her life while gaining control of yours. Under such circumstances, both you and your child display the symptoms of co-dependent behavior because, along the way, you both have adapted to each other's dysfunctional behavior. In essence, the drug-abusing child and the co-dependent parent are both addictive personalities with symptoms that are linked and that work against each other's recovery. Moreover, both child and parent take on the persona of victim.

In the beginning, the drug-abusing child becomes increasingly focused on securing and using the drug she is dependent upon. The addiction dictates the child's lifestyle and quality of life. She learns to lie, if necessary, to protect her drug supply and freedom of use. With time, this way of life undermines the child's integrity and sense of values.

Such fundamental compromises eventually cause the child a high degree of discomfort, leading her to use drugs even more in an attempt to feel better about herself. One result: The chemical-dependent child develops a higher tolerance for the drug and must use more and more. Another result: The child's life undertakes a rapid decline.

For a while, the substance-abusing child denies that there is a problem, denies that her use of drugs is out of control. But now, when the drug itself no longer provides euphoric highs, the child needs to use drugs merely to feel "normal." At the same time, the co-dependent parent has begun to focus his life on the drug-abusing child, trying as hard to prevent the child from securing and using drugs as the child does to accomplish the opposite outcome. For example, parents often try to stop the child from hanging out with undesirable friends, or try to monitor the child's every movement. Sharon, the mother in the case study in Chapter One, provides a real-life example of how some parents attempt to exert tight control over their substance-abusing children when she tells of her all-night odysseys—with baseball bat in tow—to try to stop her son from selling cocaine.

In this type of situation, one parent frequently takes on the role of peacemaker in response to the havoc wrought by the activities of the child and the other controlling parent. The peacemaking parent, however, is also a co-dependent personality because he is still reacting to what is happening around him—adapting his behavior to take on the role of good guy rather than hanging tough, drawing a line, and seeking outside help.

Co-dependent parents will seek relief from the pain of this scenario. Defense techniques include the repression of emotions as well as a full-scale effort to become the calm and collected "superparent" who is able to handle anything and everything, particularly his child's addiction. Such tactics serve the same purpose as the adolescent's increasing abuse of drugs—just like the child, the co-dependent parent is trying to anesthetize emotional pain. And just like the substance-abusing child, the parent is eventually self-driven down a road of despair.

Co-dependency, in essence, is an unconscious game played by troubled families, families that have become dysfunctional. This game has its own set of destructive rules that are seldom overtly articulated but are routinely acted out. The rules are derived from unhealthy patterns of living practiced over a number of years. We learn them from our parents and pass them along. Ironically, these rules almost always originate from the parental desire to protect the family or from an individual family member's desire to psychologically protect himself.

Despite this gloomy scenario, there is a way out of this cycle. Parents can teach themselves and their children new rules, though this requires a significant effort and the courage to shoulder some of the responsibility for what is happening with family members. Ensuing chapters will give you guidance on the specifics of this process. For now, let's look at the "rules" that you, as a co-dependent parent, are probably following.

PLAYING BY THE RULES

As the above description demonstrates, the relationship between you and your chemically addicted child is complex and not easily encapsulated. Still, research reveals there are discernible though unspoken rules that dysfunctional, co-dependent families use to cope with life. Understanding the nature of these rules and their destructive impact on the family can be a big first step for parents who want to help their children overcome drugs and who want to help themselves overcome co-dependency. The next step is changing old behavioral patterns through the development of new rules that lead to a more healthy interaction between parents and their children.

Two leading substance-abuse experts in Minnesota, John Friel, director of Counseling Associates, and Robert Subby, executive director of Family Systems Center, explain the rules associated with co-dependency this way:

> Co-dependency . . . a dysfunctional pattern of living and problem-solving . . . is nurtured by a set of rules within the family system. These rules make healthy growth and change very difficult. . . . While change is almost always risky and scary, the benefits of learning new rules are well worth it: a clear sense of self, peace of mind, and comfortable relationships.

Essentially, the following rules represent ways of protecting or isolating family members from each other and from the outside world. Further, their underlying premise is that getting too close is too risky an undertaking.

RULE #1:
IT'S NOT OKAY
TO TALK ABOUT PROBLEMS

In some families, members are repeatedly admonished not to air the family's dirty linen in public. In other families, the message is just as strong though unspoken. In such families, parents and children never talk about problems, even to one another, despite the palpable tension. Adherence to this rule eventually causes family members to avoid their own problems. This rule allows co-dependent parents to pretend their substance-abusing children are healthy and doing well. It also permits such parents to absolve themselves from blame for their children's difficulties, since problems that are not discussed are not acknowledged to exist. Yet denying problems can foster a sense of impending doom.

Feeling that disaster may lie behind any door adds another layer of stress to an already stressful situation. Co-dependent parents who are still trying to pretend nothing is wrong with their substance-abusing child become powder kegs and thus render themselves impotent, in a way, from examining options that might lead to resolution of their family's problems. Parents who have managed to dull the impact of emotional feelings through long-term denial also dull their problem-solving ability.

RULE #2:
DO NOT EXPRESS FEELINGS OPENLY

In families with unresolved chemical and co-dependency issues, emotional blocking is commonly a serious problem. Parent and child alike may come to believe that it is better to deny feelings rather than to risk letting someone else see who they really are inside. Parents who teach their children ideas like "big boys don't cry" are providing examples of this rule. With time, this suppression of a child's emotional self becomes so complete that even he no longer knows who he really is.

My sister confirms that she suffered just this type of identity crisis shortly after my mother and father separated when she was close to 14. My father insisted that she play the role of surrogate mother for our younger brother and surrogate wife for him on an emotional level. He made it clear she was supposed to help him sort out the family's financial problems and schedule day-to-day routines such as grocery shopping and menu planning. If she complained, she was made to feel guilty. So she suppressed her feelings and turned to marijuana for escape.

RULE #3:
DON'T COMMUNICATE DIRECTLY;
USE ONE PERSON AS MESSENGER

My father was guilty of this process, called triangulation, after he and my mother were divorced. He needed money but was uncomfortable asking my mother directly to help him. Instead, he told me over and over how it would be nice if my mother would help him pay the mortgage. After a while I picked up on the fact that he wanted me to take this request to my mother. Speaking indirectly in this way can cause confusion, misdirected feelings, and dishonesty. Innocent family members become victims of the inability of others to confront personal problems directly. Speaking for my father nurtured my brand of co-dependency—I like to control people and manage their lives. In this instance, I got to control both of my parents in some measure, since Father used me as a messenger and since Mother accepted my role and didn't insist that my father speak for himself.

RULE #4:
HARBOR UNREALISTIC EXPECTATIONS
FOR THE CHILD

"Be strong, good, right, perfect. Make us proud." Co-dependent families tend to deliver the message that there is only one right way to achieve these goals. Moreover, the message of perfection is: Enough is never enough. These families create an ideal about what is good or right or best, and this ideal is so far removed from reality that parents and, particularly, children end up being nagged, pushed, and criticized for not living up to the family's expectations.

My sister, for example, says, "I never wanted to go to college. I just didn't give a damn about going, but I did it because I was expected to." By the time the first summer vacation approached, she recalls, she was smoking marijuana regularly. She lasted less than two years as a college student.

RULE #5: DON'T BE SELFISH

For the co-dependent parents who preside over a family system where this rule applies, feelings of guilt are certain to emerge. Such parents learn to view themselves as wrong for placing their own needs before the needs of others. What often happens in a family of co-dependents is that one of the members tries to feel good about himself by taking care of others to such a degree that his self-esteem actually becomes dependent on these caretaking or enabling activities. Without a substance-abusing child to take care of, the co-dependent parent is left with no purpose or worth. More than one family member may take on this role, further complicating the process.

RULE #6:
DO AS I SAY, NOT AS I DO

This rule, more than any other, teaches distrust. If, for example, co-dependent parents tell their child it's bad to be a substance abuser and then use drugs themselves, the child becomes confused and suspicious. Such children learn to count only on themselves out of a need to protect themselves from the pain of inconsistency. They may also rebel against their parents' dishonesty and do the very thing they have been instructed to avoid, such as using drugs. Indeed, many children who are in drug treatment centers have parents who are themselves recovering from a chemical or alcohol addiction.

Members of a co-dependent household also tend to suffer from externalization as a result of this "Do as I say, not as I do" rule. They become second-guessers who worry too much about doing only what they think others will want them to do. Second-guessing is an extremely unstable way to live that fosters high stress levels. High stress levels can lead to a child's feeling he needs to escape. That need to escape can lead to the use of drugs.

RULE #7:
IT'S NOT OKAY TO PLAY

To play is to risk being spontaneous, and perhaps even foolish, which is too scary for the co-dependent parent. From the very beginning, co-dependent parents believe that the world is a very serious place. Life is difficult and always painful. Consequently, the child who wants to play is imprisoned in the co-dependent family. Once again, suppression of healthy desires and emotions takes place. Emotional suppression, as pointed out before, can contribute to a child's feeling a strong need to escape from the confines of the family and perhaps turn to drugs.

Despite the pathological nature of co-dependent behavior suggested by these rules, parents who are helping their children overcome drugs should keep in mind the following words of hope: These rules can and should be broken. The following chapters discuss how to map out a new set of rules to live by. You can sort out the dynamics of co-dependency and its concomitant set of rules, and your family members can develop healthy relationships.

The following case study tracks a family in such a transition. Though still displaying co-dependent behavioral patterns, this family appears to be headed along a path of recovery.

CASE STUDY:
CHRISTY, RICHARD, AND JEREMY

Christy and Richard agree that their inability to communicate has hurt their only child, 17-year-old Jeremy. The admission, however, is one of the few areas about which they have reached an accord. Thirteen years ago the couple divorced and, according to Christy, 35, few kind words have passed between the two since, especially when the topic concerns their son. "There was a lot of animosity surrounding the divorce. Richard didn't want a divorce. Richard still hates the fact that I divorced him. But I left him because I wasn't happy with the way he chose to live his life, and I thought I could be happier without him." As it turns out, she adds, "I am happier."

Richard, 38, says that once a couple has had a child it isn't a "good plan" to divorce. "I think both parents should have an opportunity to provide equal input when a child is being raised. So I think that if a couple has had a child, they should stay together no matter what—the emphasis should be on the child." The couple married when Christy was 17 and Richard 20. Four years later they were divorced. What caused the demise of the relationship? "Honestly," Richard says, "I think we just got married way, way too young."

Christy, a resident of San Jose, California, has always had legal custody of Jeremy. Over the years she has allowed her son to spend a great deal of time living in Sacramento with his father, even though she reports that Richard "drinks a lot and smokes marijuana every day." Jeremy currently lives with his dad, who confesses that he used to drink a lot but now defines himself as a social drinker who partakes only on weekends when he partakes at all. Richard is the manager of a Mercedes-Benz service center. Christy designs printed circuit boards for an electronics company. Neither Richard nor Christy has remarried.

CHRISTY

Christy feels that her ex-husband has been a bad influence on Jeremy. "He used to buy cases of Jack Daniels and take Jeremy to go play war." "Playing war" meant that Richard, Jeremy, and some of Richard's friends would take shotguns to the backcountry and just shoot. They were arrested several times for their antics. "I wanted to share more subtle, more beautiful things about life with my son," Christy says, "and it was harder to share those things when he was being enticed to shoot guns."

It didn't take Jeremy long to figure out that he could use the conflict between his parents to manipulate them to get what he wanted. Once, for example, when his mother took Jeremy's skateboard from him as a form of punishment, he demanded to move back with his father if it wasn't returned. When the skateboard was not forthcoming, he called his father, who immediately drove 300 miles to pick him up. By the time he arrived, however, Jeremy had changed his mind.

Jeremy's substance-abuse problems began when he was 12, during a one-year period when he lived with his father. Christy can still recall vividly what happened. Richard's sister was a heroin addict with a son who was four years older than Jeremy. Because of his sister's problems,

Richard had agreed to let her son live with him. "This child was already in trouble," Christy says. "So when Jeremy moved in with his dad, everything started to head rapidly downhill. Jeremy stopped going to school so that he and his cousin could party all day long while Richard held a full-time job. At one point, Jeremy had a very, very terrible acid [LSD] experience that I didn't find out about until a month later."

According to Christy, Jeremy's father dropped him off for a brief visit with the terse comment, "Jeremy's having some emotional problems; you'd better look into it." She could tell something was really wrong. "Jeremy looked so frightened, I took a week off from work and took long walks with him. We talked a lot." During one of those talks Jeremy admitted he had tried LSD, and then he started to cry. "I was livid when I found out but decided there was nothing I could do about it—the damage had been done and couldn't be undone, so I didn't say much to Richard."

Jeremy eventually returned to live with his father where, Christy complains, he was permitted to run wild. "He had no limits. His father let him do anything. Then, I think, at some point Jeremy himself was afraid of how far his father might let him go." Shortly thereafter, his father announced that Jeremy was out of control and requested that Christy take over. For the next year or so she had a hard time dealing with Jeremy. There were problems at school and at home. But toward the end of that period things were beginning to improve, so she thought it was okay to take a month-long vacation to Africa. Jeremy remained at home under the supervision of one of Christy's friends, who had agreed to house-sit as well.

When Christy returned, she discovered that Richard had dropped off a runaway friend of Jeremy's to keep him company while Christy was gone and that neither child had been attending school. As best as Christy can determine, the boys had told her friend—whose duty it was to chaperone—a number of tall tales that she had accepted at face value. The freedom the boys gained from telling the lies had allowed them to use drugs, ditch school, and, generally, engage in mayhem. Christy blamed Richard for Jeremy's setback and decided to return him to his father. Christy told her ex-husband, "I really can't be effective unless I have your support. And since I don't, I can't deal with it, so let's do it your way. Jeremy should live with you."

Today, she admits, "I think that may have been a mistake." The time spent under his father's jurisdiction ended with Jeremy's expanding his drug use to include "crystal meth," or speed, and Jeremy started to steal to support his habit. He was only 16 by the time this occurred. Eventually he was arrested for possession of stolen property and for burglary. Jeremy was released from juvenile hall to attend Spring Creek Community, a boarding school in Thompson Falls, Montana, for troubled teenagers, including substance abusers. "At Spring Creek, we were taught that it's not just the child with a problem, it's the family that has a problem."

Christy believes that she tried harder than did her ex-husband and son to break the many patterns of dysfunctional behavior that continue to plague her family, such as Richard's tendency to come to Jeremy's rescue at the drop of a hat and her desire to want to "fix things" for Jeremy. "Richard," she says, "didn't cooperate with Jeremy's counselor at Spring Creek whatsoever." Further, she adds, "Jeremy didn't like his counselor because the counselor is a very strong figure. He's physically big and he's a no-nonsense type of person and he wouldn't let Jeremy get away with things—and Jeremy likes to get away with things."

She got the most out of the year Jeremy stayed at Spring Creek, she feels, because she made the biggest effort to participate in the group family sessions conducted there. Jeremy has been drug-free for about a year now. He currently lives with his father and works part-time for a fast-food operation. He attends school and is doing very well according to Christy, who hears from him by telephone once every week or two. Still, Christy has her doubts: "I have mixed feelings about how well Jeremy is doing, in part because I think he might be paying me lip service. But I do see some improvement, though I don't know how long this is going to last. So I am not very happy with the way this family has turned out. But I am happy with my life, and what I really want is for Jeremy to be happy with his life."

RICHARD

"It's real easy for a twelve-year-old to get drugs nowadays," Richard points out while explaining that Jeremy first started using marijuana by purchasing it from other children at school. "If a kid has five bucks, he can get just about any kind of drug he wants at his local high school. It's a real, drastic problem for parents to deal with right now."

Richard knew his son was using drugs because he recognized many of the signs. "All of a sudden Jeremy wanted to sleep in in the mornings. His attention span wasn't normal. And he didn't care about anything anymore. We tried to talk about what was going on, but it didn't work out. Soon he got way out of control, so I sent him back to his mother."

This pattern of Jeremy's moving back and forth between his mother and father during times of crisis continued for a few years, Richard acknowledges. As Jeremy grew older, however, his behavior grew worse. "Jeremy would just go away and stay with friends for four or five days at a time," Richard remembers. "It was past due for me to be an authority figure, but just before he finally ran away from me I saw that he refused to accept my authority."

It was during this period that Jeremy was arrested. "I thought the kid he was hanging out with was a kid. But later I found out the guy was twenty-three years old. I was shocked. He looked so young." It turns out that this man made a practice of preying on teenagers who had drug problems, getting them involved in burglary schemes to support their habits and to support himself. Explains Richard: "They got caught when they broke into my neighbor's house—only two doors down from me—in broad daylight with the neighbor at home. On April 13, 1987, that's when Jeremy went to juvenile hall."

By mid-June of that year, Jeremy was enrolled in Spring Creek. Richard likes some things about the school but does not like the "methods they use for therapy." He likes the school's Survival Course, which requires the children to hike as much as 100 miles over a three-week period and to manage with very little food. They are expected to live off the land. On the other hand, Richard does not like the way the parent group meetings are conducted. He feels that he's being pressured to not question the school and to become emotional. Richard is uncomfortable being put into either of those positions.

"These parent therapy sessions are very emotional. The counselor really tries to break a person down. It worked on Christy. After a while she did whatever the school said she should do about how to deal with Jeremy. Five years ago, she wouldn't have taken some of the positions she took with Jeremy." Still, Richard tried to go along with the program when Jeremy's counselor suggested the father "get some goals going for Jeremy." So, according to Richard, he and Jeremy made a deal: If Jeremy made excellent grades in the upcoming semester, he could go to Hawaii in the summer.

Inspired, Jeremy earned the grades, but he also broke the school's rules by putting two tattoos on the calf of his right leg: a skull with thorns sticking out and a skeleton of a bull that has big, ugly teeth. Richard recalls that his first thought was, "Why did Jeremy do this? Why wasn't he being supervised?" Jeremy's counselor suggested that the Hawaiian trip be cancelled. Christy agreed; Richard did not.

From Richard's point of view, his agreement to take Jeremy to Hawaii was based on the child's academic performance alone. As far as his grades went, Jeremy had done well, so Richard saw no need to renege on the trip. "I told Christy, 'There's no way I am going to tell Jeremy to his face that he can't go. There's no way I can turn my back on him. There's no way I can do that. It would make Jeremy feel so alone.'" Richard removed Jeremy from Spring Creek and they went to Hawaii.

Jeremy returned from the trip to live with his father. Within two days he got a job and has been saving to pay the insurance costs and repairs on an old car he has purchased. Because of the time he missed from school while using drugs, Jeremy's education is only at the tenth-grade level. Richard and Jeremy are looking into adult education programs that will allow Jeremy to attend school part-time, working toward a General Education Diploma (GED).

Jeremy has decided to become a lawyer. Richard also proudly relates that his drug-free son "gets on me about smoking cigarettes."

JEREMY

"I took drugs because I had so much fun doing it. But when you come down [after using drugs] you don't feel good, so you use drugs to feel better," 17-year-old Jeremy points out. "I was around eleven years old when I first started using drugs. I didn't think about it too much because everybody I hung around with used drugs." Jeremy started smoking marijuana after coming to live with his father and a 16-year-old cousin. It was this cousin who introduced Jeremy to drugs.

By the time he was 13, Jeremy says, "I was doing all kinds of drugs—LSD, opium, and mushrooms. My dad knew I was using drugs by the time I was in the eighth grade, but at first he didn't think that there was any problem with it." When asked why he was so sure his father knew what was going on, Jeremy explains, "He knew after a while because we talked about it." During this period Jeremy returned to live with his mother.

"Then she went on vacation to Africa right when one of my friends had been kicked out by his parents. He was fourteen years old and had no place to go, so I let him stay with me. He slept in the garage, and the lady who was supposed to be looking after me while my mother was gone never knew that my friend was really living in the garage. When my mother came back she found out right away. She called my dad and said she didn't even want me back. So I lived with my dad, and by then I was out of control."

He used methamphetamine regularly. "It keeps you

awake. I would stay up for three or four days at a time and then come home and sleep for hours and hours." Jeremy admits that he broke into houses and into cars to support his drug habit. He also sold stolen marijuana. "People in this part of California grow a lot of marijuana plants during the summer. You can smell where they're growing, so we would just sneak over fences and steal enough of the plant to sell a pound or more at a time. We made a lot of money." A pound of stolen marijuana plants would sell for $1,600, "give or take $200." Jeremy was 14 at the time.

Soon Jeremy was arrested for burglary. "My dad got me out and they let me off, but between two weeks and a month later I got caught with stolen merchandise. The stuff was in my garage. I was put in juvenile hall for two months." Eventually he was released to attend Spring Creek Community.

Jeremy thinks that the school was especially tough. "They [Spring Creek counselors] play a lot of head games. They say things like, 'We have total control over you.' 'You're not going to get out of here until you deal with your parents.'" He describes the specific counselor assigned to him as "cold-blooded and ruthless. Seriously, I didn't trust him. Once he picked me and two friends up and told us we were going skiing. Then he drove us to the middle of nowhere and we had to hike for four days. We ate one meal a day—a bowl of rice—and slept in sleeping bags without tents in seventeen-degree weather."

To defy authority, Jeremy says, he tattooed himself. "I just decided that it was something that I could do that they couldn't do anything about." At the time, Jeremy says, he didn't like anything about Spring Creek. Now, he acknowledges, "What I think I got out of it was it kept me sober long enough to think about what I was doing with my life." Jeremy left Spring Creek in August 1988. Currently he lives with his father in Sacramento. He calls his mother regularly and believes his life has taken a definite turn for the better.

"Things are a lot easier now. I don't have to worry about everything. When I see a sheriff, I don't have to worry. And now that I'm sober, I can think about what I want my life to be like and try to make the best happen. I'm going to AA [Alcoholics Anonymous] meetings two or three times a week. It keeps me thinking right. After I finish high school I want to go to college and then law school." Asked if it is hard for him to stay away from drugs, Jeremy says, "Once you're on the path it's easy not to use drugs. It's harder to get on the path."

POSTSCRIPT

"Jeremy is a chronically dependent young man," reports his former counselor at Spring Creek, who asked to go unnamed. "By his own reports Jeremy used methamphetamine, marijuana, and alcohol. He's a polydrug user." Jeremy's history was that he would stay with his mother until he was bored, then would go live with his father. But, the counselor notes, "whenever criminality took place, the father, in frustration and unknowingness, would call the mother and say, 'I don't know what to do—take over.'

"Richard doesn't want to be the 'bad guy', that's his terminology," the counselor adds. As proof he cites the way Jeremy addressed his parents in letters. "Jeremy referred to his father in correspondence as 'Yo Dude.' Letters to his mother had a very different and more respectful tone." On the other hand, the counselor surmised that Christy's difficulty with co-dependence had to do with some unresolved feelings and anger around her divorce. "It's impossible for her to take a bottom-line stand with Richard. Though in the last meeting before Richard removed Jeremy from the school she did get tough," the counselor recalls.

"Richard," he says, "is a very pleasant person over the phone. He appears to be compassionate. But in person he demonstrates something else. His conflict style is passive-aggressive." One example the counselor gives involves an evening when Richard drove to the school and picked Jeremy up without saying anything to anybody. He returned Jeremy seven days later, in the middle of the night. Richard tended to avoid face-to-face meetings with Spring Creek staff, the counselor notes, so he didn't take part in many of the parent group meetings. Christy did take part, "in a very independent and healthy way."

"Jeremy was looking at one year solid incarceration time when the Spring Creek intervention took place," the counselor says. At Spring Creek, Jeremy bonded with the subgroups, or children on the fringes of "punk" culture. Still, the counselor reports, "Jeremy was quite a playful and pleasant person to be around when engaged in sports activities. But when confronted with task completion he became sullen and withdrawn."

The counselor has a somewhat different point of view than Richard of the Hawaiian vacation that led to Jeremy's departure from Spring Creek. "In some way I take exception that Richard took Jeremy away, because that action implies that he [Jeremy] was faced with some evil presence. The entire counseling treatment team recommended that Jeremy not go to Hawaii but that Richard and Jeremy spend time together on the campus. We asked him [Richard], 'Do you want to reinforce Jeremy's negative behavior by rewarding him with a vacation?" Richard said no, but by the time he arrived to see Jeremy, he had changed his mind."

Jeremy had a tattoo on his hand before arriving at Spring Creek. During his tenure at the school, the counselor says, Jeremy made a tattoo gun and placed additional tattoos on himself and other students.

The counselor forecasts a fairly circumscribed future for Jeremy unless he receives long-term treatment. "I think Jeremy's problem with intimacy will plague him for quite some time. He has difficulty with trust, with boundaries. I think Jeremy will suffer from episodic relapses that will result in incarceration unless professional treatment is sought and both he and his father abide by that advice."

Both Christy and Richard express regrets about their roles in Jeremy's downfall. "When he was so terribly strung out on acid," Christy recalls, "he was like a blank canvas. I remember thinking that at the time. When a person's in that condition you can do almost anything with him to direct him in the right direction. Boy, I wish I had done something then." But, she says, she returned him to his father because "I didn't want to rescue Jeremy. That's one of his problems." Christy feels that if she had been stronger and could have afforded to send him to a boarding school sooner, she might have been able to help Jeremy. However, she laments, "The money [from having increased her income over the years] came too late."

Richard feels he failed Jeremy by not showing his son "where the buck stops. Just doing that would have been the most important thing for Jeremy. Parents are the only real guidance children have. But I didn't like being a disciplinarian." Things appear to be different now. As Richard describes it, he and Jeremy "have a talk once a week where we both get to say whatever is bothering us. Jeremy also is required, every night, to make a list of whatever he plans to do the next day. Jeremy thinks it's a 'retarded idea,' but it's one of my new rules, and it's something he has to live with."

Clearly, Christy and Richard displayed co-dependent behavior by playing into Jeremy's manipulations and thus enabling him to use drugs and miss school. But is Richard's concern over not having drawn a stricter line with Jeremy a reasonable concern? Did the strict lines Christy drew help or hurt Jeremy? Such questions are examined in the following chapter, "Hanging Tough."

⚘ 3 ⚘

Hanging Tough

Hanging tough may be the right thing to do when dealing with a drug-dependent family member, but it certainly is not the easy thing to do. I learned this lesson a few years ago when my cocaine-addicted sister came to live with me. Hanging tough involved giving up my co-dependent desire to rescue her, and it also involved drawing a line, establishing boundaries beyond which I would not allow her to cross. To do so was particularly difficult for me because I felt as if I was being selfish. What I didn't know then but have since come to understand is that being selfish under such circumstances is okay.

For years I had carried around a powerful image of my sister: She was my live paper doll. As a child she had been very cute, very smart, and quite personable. I found pleasure in buying her beautiful clothes and jewelry during her adolescent years. So when she arrived on my doorstep in her mid-twenties bedraggled and in need of financial and emotional support, I was quick to come to the rescue. In retrospect, her drug problem should have been easy to spot. But at first I simply could not come to grips with the new image of the young woman who stood before me.

As my sister's behavior deteriorated and I finally had

to face the fact that she was addicted to rock cocaine, another complication arose that prevented me from taking swift and decisive action against her: I found out she was pregnant, intended to keep the child, and was not necessarily going to get married. I remember saying over and over again in conversations with my best friend, "How can I put my pregnant sister out into the streets?"

Though my sister remained employed up until her sixth month of pregnancy, she could account for less and less of her money as her cocaine addiction grew worse. Toward the end of her tenure at my home she no longer set aside money for food or transportation to and from her job. Instead, she relied on me, other family members, and friends to meet her most basic needs. And for a long time we all came through for her. After all, how could anyone let an unmarried, pregnant woman starve?

Despite warnings from my friends that for my own good I had to ask my sister to leave, I continued to try to "help" and she continued to use drugs. Eventually, the situation peaked when I discovered that my sister had made many more long-distance calls on my telephone than she could afford, and that a drug dealer had begun to visit my household regularly. I banned the dope peddler from my home, was stuck with an expensive telephone bill, and faced a tough decision I could not escape: Her pregnancy notwithstanding, my sister had to go.

Hanging tough for me was watching my sister leave, knowing that she had burned her bridges and had nowhere to go. She ended up spending some time in a shelter for the homeless before she finally gave up cocaine and had a healthy child. It was a long time before I could leave my guilt behind and believe that my choice had been the right one.

My guilt and pain reemerged a year later, when my

sister found out I was working on this book and we sat down to talk about what had happened during those troublesome days. What I found out was that I had failed her in some significant way by drawing the line so late in the game. Just as she had wanted my father to tell her no, she had wanted me to tell her to stop using drugs:

> Dad could have asked some very pointed questions, he could have followed me, but he didn't and I know why he didn't: Dad was too wrapped up in his own problems. He was worrying about his marriage coming to an end. So the most he did for me was the obligatory things to do, but his heart wasn't in it. He never asked that I leave a phone number of where I was going to be, for example. And if he wasn't going to ask any questions, I wasn't going to volunteer any information. Since I was only fourteen or fifteen years old, I took advantage of the situation, though I don't know too many fourteen- or fifteen-year-olds who wouldn't have.

It was hard for me to hear my sister's depiction of what had happened with my father, because she hit too close to home. I, too, had neglected to ask my sister the necessary "pointed questions." Over and over again my sister has told me in our recent discussions that she had wanted my help, she had wanted me to ask her why she was doing these things to herself. She still doesn't quite understand what took me so long to decide to hang tough.

SETTING PRIORITIES: FIRST THINGS FIRST

I tend to disagree with my sister's beliefs about why our father chose to remain quiet while she abused drugs, based on my own reactions to her drug problem. I didn't move as fast as I could have because I was scared that to draw a line would indicate a lack of tolerance and, thus, a lack of love on my part. Understanding what I understand now, as well as no longer being in the middle of the fray, I can see more clearly that such a point of view was yet another reflection of my co-dependent behavior. By caring about what cutting my sister off might "indicate" to others, I was really serving as my sister's enabler: I was more concerned about my own image than in helping her overcome drugs.

These days, I also recognize that my co-dependency involved playing the martyr's role. As long as my sister stuck around and abused my hospitality, I could feel superior by showing that I could handle the worst of situations with strength and perseverance. I have since learned that hanging tough—accepting the legitimacy of the boundaries I set, acknowledging that some behavior is intolerable indeed—was the appropriate thing to do, for my sister and for myself.

Admittedly, hanging tough—through setting the priority that you must take care of yourself first—is a scary and guilt-provoking step for many parents. I worried many nights over how my sister was faring. And I have certainly spent many nights lamenting my co-dependent behavior that, in some ways, nurtured my sister's chemical dependency by postponing her inevitable fall. Having experienced what I experienced, it's easy for me to relate to why Richard, the father in Chapter Two's case study, allowed his son to run rampant for so long before seeking outside help. In light of what has happened, his ex-wife's tendency to regret her more hard-line approach—to insist that her son make his own decisions and, thus, not intervene—is also not too difficult to understand.

According to Steven W. Cawdrey, headmaster and co-founder of Montana's Spring Creek Community, "Traditionally we've been raised to believe that selfishness is self-centeredness. Self-centeredness is dysfunctional and a characteristic of co-dependency; selfishness is not." Cawdrey points out that it is healthy to say to your substance-abusing child, "I will not be treated this way; I don't deserve it." Interestingly enough, by taking such actions and thus taking care of yourself first, you are also helping your troubled child. "Addictive personalities have to get other people and institutions to buy into their behavior in order to actively engage in co-dependency," Cawdrey notes. Setting clear boundaries, then, is the appropriate way to deal with your child who is using drugs. "If you create boundaries, a person has to face himself in the mirror. Always, always, always, a diseased person should be faced with what you are observing about his behavior and asked to make a choice to either change or continue practicing the disease."

So, as difficult as it might be, parents who help their children overcome drugs have to learn how to hang tough, to set priorities, and be prepared to handle their own symptoms of co-dependency such as their need to rescue, to enable, to believe that it's not okay to take care of themselves first. On my own, I eventually sought the services of a psychologist. Most reputable drug-treatment programs include counseling for all members of the family on an individual and group basis. Some programs virtually require that at least one parent get involved in the treatment program.

Cawdrey advises the parents of addicted children who attend his residential facility to prioritize their efforts to maintain themselves and their family in the following way:

1. Work on Stabilizing Your Relationship with Yourself

What are your needs? What are your limits? What do you understand and what don't you understand about what's going on? Make sure you can honestly answer such questions.

2. Work on Stabilizing Your Relationship with Your Spouse or Significant Other

Are you ignoring your spouse in order to deal with problems caused by your child's drug abuse? What about the family's finances? Has your spouse had to sacrifice a long-saved-for purchase to pay the legal fees of your troubled child?

3. Work on Stabilizing the Lives of the Other Members of the Family Unit, Including Siblings as Well as the Young Substance Abuser

Have you noticed whether a sister or brother who is not on drugs is having problems with schoolwork? Is the sibling who shares a bedroom with the substance-abusing child being pressured as well to use drugs? Is the troubled child stealing from the sibling?

4. Take Care That You Don't Harm Your Relationships with People at Your Workplace by Your Reaction to Familial Stresses

Are you arguing with your co-workers more frequently than ever before? Is your work product showing signs of deterioration? Have you become unreliable or unpredictable so that your subordinates or superiors are beginning to complain to you and to others?

EASIER SAID THAN DONE—
BUT WORTH THE TROUBLE

As simple as this prescription for recovery is, it is not always easy to follow. Parents typically find it hard to put themselves first when their substance-abusing child consistently maneuvers to be rescued from potentially critical situations—and not-so-critical situations. Jeremy, the teenager discussed in the last chapter's case study, provides a prime example.

As you'll recall, when his mother, Christy, took away his skateboard to punish him for some inappropriate deed, he called his father to come and get him. Richard dropped what he was doing and drove for three hours to pick up his son—without calling Christy to clarify Jeremy's claims—only to find that Jeremy had changed his mind by the time his father arrived.

Richard felt that "hanging tough"—to stay put and let Jeremy deal with his problem on his own—would have been less than helpful to his son. He believed that coming to Jeremy's rescue was the proper thing to do. Richard's co-dependent behavior involved a need to be a "buddy" to Jeremy rather than an authority figure. Ironically, however, the message Jeremy received from his father's rescuing actions undermined his confidence in himself. It was a message that said, "You can't deal with your own problems. You're incompetent. You're weak." By consistently hanging tough, on the other hand, Richard would have encouraged Jeremy to face the direct consequences of his actions. In dealing with unpleasant situations on his own, Jeremy would have developed the experience and maturity that lead to feelings of self-confidence and pride.

Hanging tough with a drug-abusing child, and thus giving your own needs first consideration, poses special problems in dealing with a spouse. The other parent may not yet recognize the wisdom of refusing to rescue an addicted child and will continue to do so, even when experience has demonstrated that rescuing does not help. Some parents have gone so far as to financially and emotionally bankrupt the family in order to "save" the addicted adolescent.

While Cawdrey's four-pronged guidelines for parents who are trying to help their children overcome drugs may not be easy to follow, for those parents who accept the challenge, there is hope in knowing that these guidelines can produce successful results. Adhering to these guidelines can also serve as a basis for helping parents to rewrite the rules of co-dependency outlined in Chapter Two:

Rule #1: It's not okay to talk about problems.

Rule #2: Do not express feelings openly.

Rule #3: Don't communicate directly; use one person as messenger.

Rule #4: Harbor unrealistic expectations for the child.

Rule #5: Don't be selfish.

Rule #6: Do as I say, not as I do.

Rule #7: It's not okay to play.

Taking a hanging-tough approach to dealing with your child requires revision of the first three rules in order to create boundaries, to draw lines. As a parent who is hanging tough, you must confront your substance-abusing child with the behavioral problems you have observed. This process requires you to express your feelings of distress openly and directly to your child. Moreover, unrealistic expectations for your child (Rule #4) have no place in the hanging-tough scenario. What's at issue is the choice your child is prepared to take, *on her own,* between abusing drugs and living a full life. As described by Cawdrey, "Children who use drugs need to be forced to make one of two conscious decisions: either (1) they continue to practice using drugs, which is choosing to die, or (2) they are willing to ask for help, which is choosing to live." Expecting your child to opt for one of these choices is not unrealistic.

As for Rule #5, remember, hanging tough means that you understand the benefits to yourself and to your substance-abusing child of looking out for number one first. Rule #6 is inoperable when a parent is attempting to hang tough; such hypocrisy and dishonesty are the antithesis of a hanging-tough approach. When you draw lines and establish boundaries you are, by definition, letting your child know precisely what you will and will not tolerate. You are insisting that neither you nor your child will cut any corners. Your message is not ambiguous, as is the case with a parent who is laboring under the "Do as I say, not as I do" mode of behavior.

The last rule involves the suppression of emotions. Again, this rule violates the basic premise of hanging tough. As a parent, you need to let your child know what you are feeling and, in addition, you want your child to communicate in an equally straightforward way what is on her mind and what is in her heart.

The next chapter will introduce a concept called "raising the bottom," the second phase of the hanging-tough concept. It explains how establishing an intervention method can cause your child to feel as if she has hit rock bottom although, in truth, a safety net is in place. For now, however, Eve and Mickey's story provides another opportunity to see how hanging-tough can be put to work. Every family is different, so don't expect neat and clean solutions—results of that kind are simply unrealistic.

This family has two adolescent sons who have used drugs and two daughters who have not. The youngest son refused to be interviewed for this book. He recently ran away from boarding school and currently lives outside the home. His parents believe he is still using drugs. The oldest son, who has since recovered enough from his use of drugs to attend college, agreed to share his experiences. The father declined to allow the daughters to participate in this project. Much of Frank's tale (the son who refused to participate) is told by his mother, Eve, and by his stepbrother, Mike.

CASE STUDY:
EVE, MICKEY, MIKE, AND FRANK

When Eve and Mickey married nine years ago, it was the second time around for both. Each brought children to the newly established family, so they expected some complications. What they eventually had to cope with, however, is quite another matter. Mike, Mickey's 19-year-old son, began using drugs and basically kept the house in an uproar, according to both Eve and Mickey. "When I came home I never knew what was going to hit me in the face," Mickey says. Eve's son, Frank, 17, also contributed to the family disorder by lying, stealing, and abusing drugs.

The activities of Mike and Frank "threatened the new marriage," Mickey reports. The boys' behavior also affected the couple's two younger children: Laurie, 13, Eve's daughter from her former marriage and Frank's sister; and 16-year-old Amy, Mickey's daughter and Mike's sister. "Laurie does not trust males," states Eve, "and Amy feels the great loss of never having had a real relationship with her brother." The family lives in a large home in a suburb of Charlotte, North Carolina. Eve, 40, is a housewife, though she worked earlier in the marriage; Mickey, 46, is a real estate appraiser.

EVE

Frank's problems started to show up in the sixth grade, Eve recalls, when he was living with her ex-husband, who had remarried. "Frank was signing his stepmother's name to report cards and school papers. He was stealing from both households—his father's and mine. And Frank would lie a lot, but if later he was caught he would say that you had misunderstood what he had said." In addition, Eve says, "Earlier on Frank had acted out sexually with his sister and younger brother [from his father's second marriage]."

Frank came to live with Eve and Mickey in June of 1986 because his stepmother had had two miscarriages, which she felt were brought on by the stress of having to deal with Frank. Eve agreed to the move because Frank conned her into believing that he was being treated unfairly at his father's home. "I accepted his story hook, line, and sinker. But what Frank really wanted was a more liberal household. I'm more open than his father, who's an extreme disciplinarian and who doesn't believe in therapy."

Two weeks after he arrived at her home, Frank was caught with marijuana. "In my household there are no cigarettes even, because I'm allergic to smoke. So when I smelled the pot Frank had been smoking, I knew that something was going on. I searched his room and found the proof of what I was suspecting. When I confronted Frank, he tried to lie to get out of trouble, but, of course, we knew he wasn't telling the truth." As it turned out, Frank's use of marijuana was only the beginning of many behavioral problems.

"Frank took a fire extinguisher and sprayed it inside the sanctuary of the church," Eve recalls. He also "rocked a car" (threw rocks at a vehicle) because "he thought it would be a fun thing to do," Eve says with some exasperation. "He was acting out sexually with a lot of girls, including a girl who was twelve and the daughter of an FBI agent. Frank was fifteen at the time. He would steal my car at night to go out with the girl. The girl's father was threatening to bring charges against Frank, but that didn't seem to faze Frank one bit. He continued to sneak around with the girl."

Frank stole money from Eve that she assumed she had spent, and by tenth grade he was cutting school more than he was attending classes. But at home, Eve remembers, "Frank was personable and easy to get along with, if you could accept that he rarely told the truth. Frank's the kind of person who can steal from you but you still love him to death." During this period Frank graduated in his drug use to taking speed, LSD, and, Eve and Mickey suspected, cocaine. Eve sought outside help from a therapist and discovered that Frank has a borderline personality disorder that she describes this way: "He's stuck in doing things that show intense rebellion. He refuses to accept that he cannot get anything that he wants at whatever price he has to pay, or whatever price someone else has to pay."

After repeated warnings from the FBI agent about his affair with the 12-year-old daughter, Frank scooped the girl